Expressed Requiem

Rebecca Marie

Presentation by *BookLeaf Publishing*

Web: www.bookleafpub.com

E-mail: info@bookleafpub.com

ISBN: 9789357748209

First edition 2023

This particular orbit around the sun has been a significantly poignant year for me. For that reason, I am owning everyone from here on out and graciously accept the next one.

My Peanut is growing into a beautiful young woman and our relationship is taking on new adventures. We talk about boys, the cycle of life, religion, ornery friends, rough days at school, and finish almost every evening with a quick cuddle. I have a beautiful bond with my daughter that I have only ever read about in a book, and I am truly honored to have the experience.

I have no idea what the future holds or for how long, but I do know that we all end up at the same destination. In the meantime, I've learned to grab each moment by the horns, ride it like the boss you are, and don't forget to make memories.

Stay kind and humble. Agree to disagree and look at situations from opposing viewpoints.

Sadly, there are people I had to walk away from. Sometimes you are unable to see where someone is coming from, no matter how much yoga you do. Before you walk, just make sure you say your peace as kindly as possible, regardless of the outcome. It's always worth it.

And love -

Fickle, tumultuous love, with its euphoric highs and epic lows. My ride or dies, my road dogs. Relationships are truly a lifelong hustle. We adult as best we can, sometimes winging it, yet continue to do so.

Thank you <3

ACKNOWLEDGEMENT

That peace is going to cost you.

Your family.
Your relationship.
Your friends.
Your career.
Even the ghosts of your former self.

Your reward is a new life…
Keep going.

So I wrote.

1994

I've seen some funny people,
With laughter in their eyes,
And the tears of sorrowness.

What can we do?
Can we turn back time?
But think of all the things we would have to
leave behind.

1995

Friends are two flowers that flourish in the
summer sun,
Ever so bright and beautiful.

They are touched with a light, delicate scent,
Reminding you of tender memories once shared.

When the whispering wind comes dancing
through the fields,
It is the two friends sharing intimate secrets.

When the pelting rains of winter freeze you
solid,
And the gusting wind blows your dainty stalk,
It is a friend that is there for you,
Kindling a fire that makes the fiercest blizzards
wither away into nothing.

Unlike a flower though,
Friends do not ease away like the coming of the
day or rising of the night.

They are there forever.

1996

Look into my eyes, my friend,
Tell me what you see.
Do you see the one who cries,
"You were meant for me?!"
Look into my eyes, my friend,
I'll follow you anywhere.
Time with you is magical,
Can't you see I care?

1997

I'm sick of this game of cat and mouse.
I either have you, or you run away.

These limbs are not as agile as they once were,
For time has taken the need to go get you.

This mind is not as sharp as it once was,
For your hurting words dulled my happiness.

These claws are not as strong as they once were,
For I haven't the strength to hold on and they're
breaking.

My heart doesn't beat and give me the energy
that I need,
For you've broken it and it's not healing.

Sagittarius

Your smile –
Tells me everything will be alright.

Your hands –
Grasp mine and hold me tight.

Your words –
Are endearing ones, always knowing.

Just like your love –
A river, forever flowing.

Chance and coincidence brought us together,
Similarities made us friends.

What's between us is to be treasured,
It is my love I send.

Taurus

The stare we used to share across the room
Is now a gaze right before we kiss.

Our laughs over jokes and drinks
Has turned into giggles when we find each
other's sweet spots.

Hugs we gave before we departed
Is now the embrace that holds me through the
night.

Somewhere in between time and friendship
We came together and became one.

2005

Once there was a little dude that thought the Army sucked.
He fell out of bed and hit his face on the bottom bunk.

"Oh crap," he said and stifled a laugh.
"This Army thing is not going to last."

He picked himself up and started to walk,
When his Sergeant came over to have a little talk.

'Look here son," he started to say,
"Stop fumbling with yourself, the troops think you're gay."

"Oh no," said the private as he grimaced in pain.
"I promise you, the divorce did not make me that way."

He grabbed his loofah and skipped off to the shower,
When another big Sarge came and stood over him like a tower.

"Do you need any help, like maybe a sponge
bath?"
The little dude just puckered, and ran away fast.

He did away with the shower and put his
uniform on,
The Army was a place he definitely didn't
belong.

Next was chow, although it made his stomach
churn,
The milk was always chunky and the soup was
too firm.

After that was formation, where he always got
barked at.
His boots were too big and his BDUs made him
look fat.

"Rollie Pollie you need a pt test," the First
Sergeant said.
"I don't care if you can't run and wind up dead."

"Sure," said the troop, standing up more straight,
This Army thing was becoming something to
hate.

2014

I forget. I keep forgetting. That I don't have the
final say in things, that my opinion is not
wanted, and when asked, it still doesn't weigh in.
I am to be the silent, agreeable side who should
just be eternally grateful and humbled that you
even want to still be around me.
I'm naughty. I talk. I curse. I care, even when I
know I really shouldn't.
So here's to the arm candy, the silent halves, the
waifs of human beings who echo who they once
were and have become scared of their own
shadow.
Blended, I go back to my corner.

P.S. Fuck you.

2016

You grow up to become what you're told,
Only to grow up and change again.

Beauty is told to those who behold,
Only to learn that they are nothing.

Sacrifice and honor, told to be bold,
Only in the eyes of the deceiver.

Honor your creases, follow the fold,
Only to rumple and fall away.

2017

I used to think addiction was like a mask. That you could float in and out of the highs and lows, reaching the person when they are sober and lucid. Sometimes making a difference, sometimes not. Forever hopeful that the mask would come permanently off and they could breathe fresh air again.

The reality is, it has become molded onto their face and never comes off. There is literally nothing you can do about it.

And, dammit. I miss you. You're standing right next to me and I don't even know who you are anymore.

Harm

At first it was a smack.
Not a really hard one, mind you. Just enough to startle, and make her compliant.
But as her will grew, so did the pain.
And as the hits became harder, so did she.
She steadied herself, embraced the impact, and rubbed the pain away until the redness disappeared.
Next, it was a pinprick.
But it didn't really draw any blood, so it was rather tolerable.
Then, when that first drop of red rose to the surface, she was a little surprised.
And after it kept happening, she would just smear the drop away and continue on with her day.
Naturally, the pricks turned into knife slashes.
And as the wounds became deeper, they became septic.
Some days, pain skipped infliction.
She didn't know what to do with herself, since it felt so abnormal.
So as she healed, she would pick at the scabs herself, just to draw blood.
Occasionally, swirling for resonance.

Words.
Those were the ones that hurt the most.
And the saddest part of all, is that she actually
believed them.
It was always her fault. She was never enough.
Her attempts were unworthy. Trying her best
was the equivalent of not trying.
Even being compliant, she was accused of being
a rebel.
Then, one day unexpectedly, even to herself, she
shattered.
Imploded, really.
And after the initial impact and numbing
upheaval, she slowly put herself back together.
Without saying anything, she chose which pieces
to rebuild herself with.
Some days she couldn't choose, so she sat in
quiet solitude, while the hits kept on coming.
Other days, she awoke with an unquenchable
determination and grabbed multiple pieces in
supernatural knowing.
And then there were weeks where there was
nothing but silence and soulful contemplation as
she rearranged the pieces.
The whole time, other pieces were left behind on
the floor.
Never once touched, eternally dismissed.
A single glance, and they were left behind
forever.

You do not know this new her.
And you shouldn't.

Woke

One day, you wake up, embraced by the sun.
At first, the intensity is so blindingly brilliant
you can't see.
It hurts, this unaccustomed light.
Yet the warmth feels familiarly comfortable.
And as you relax and ease into it, both eyes
adjust.
Your muscles warm up and stretch your bones
back into place.
Realigning into your soul.
Everything feels right in your world again.
You lounge, basking in the sunlight.
Remembering who you once were without the
darkness of the past.
Before the pain, the suffering, or the ego.
The past will come calling.
Do not answer, it will leave.
The memories will come back.
Do not dwell, they will fade.
The temptations will rise.
Do not submit, they will subside.
The people will try to reenter,
Do not yield, let them float away.
No one said it was going to be hard.
But it will get easier.

No one said there would be tears.
But they will dry.
No one said there will be heartache.
But it will heal.
When practice becomes perfection,
When that darkness comes knocking,
When the antagonists try to embrace,
And you get tired and tempted to fall down
again –
You will recognize that letting go was the
hardest part.
You will persevere because it is all that you
know.
You will stay the course because there is no
other.
You will continue to live in the light, because
you can never go back.
And it will get easier.

Every.

Single.

Time.

Leo

You will find in nature,
A particular spot.
One that is comfortable.
One that you can relax in.
One that invites your thoughts.
As you frequent,
As you become one.
You will also be accepted.
The trees will talk through the creaks from their
boughs.
The birds will sing you their lullabies.
The grass will embrace, letting you sink in.
Even the insects will occasionally caress and
kiss your skin.
Will you silence your mind and listen?
Will you drop your guard and allow?
Will you release and receive?
Every day, just a little bit more.

2018

Ownership,
Without commitment.

I'm starting to think,
That if this is the standard,
If this is the way of the world ...

If.
If this is unromanticized reality,
That no one breathes a word about,
Yet we all silently suffer and accept ...

Fuck the human condition.

My respect is earned not given.
Kindness is not flirting.
Politeness isn't cheating.
Breathing isn't selfishness.
Self-care isn't a luxury.

So, with that,
I'll be over here.
By myself.
It was lonely at first,
And I was very tired.

Until I got to know myself.
Until I replenished my soul.

Now conversating is too noisy.
And I'd rather wrap myself in solitude.
Celebrating waking up every morning.
Creating my visions.
Grateful for freedom.
Excited for new adventures.
Thanking the universe for another day.
Another moment.

So if you too,
Find yourself tired.
Drained.
Having enough.
Come sit with me.
In silent solidarity,
Of what could be,
And of what is yet to come.

2019

Empty promises are where dreams go to
hibernate,
As the little girl inside wishes, "Not again."

Usury comes in many forms,
As it's whispered in her ear, "I need you."

Both feet, finding yourself jumping in,
As she remembered the old lover whispering,
"No regrets."

Missing bad habits is okay,
Just don't pick them up again.

Single Mom

"You've changed…"
"I had to."
"We used to …"
"I'm not a housewife anymore."
"I need more…"
"I'm giving you what I have."

It is an ever-delicate balance of
Friend
Lover
Coworker
Patient
Child
Then there is the inner world of
Single parent
Compromised immune
Housework
Fur babies
Side hustle
Muse
Self Care
To Do
Constantly rotating
Frequent check-ins
Adjusting fire

Sheer exhaustion

All to have
Independence
Happiness
Freedom and
Peace

It's actually very expensive,
with no price tag.
I'm dancing as fast as I can
Yet they are still complaining
So it's time for another change
Reluctantly,
Begrudgingly,
Hesitatingly,
Again.
The give and take…

You can't pour from an empty cup.
So -
It's time to
Drink.

And Savor.

Phoenix

When I first started this journey I was devastated and then raged.

"Make it all burn."

And so it did.
Gloriously.
Epicly.

And now, I look at these ashes and embers too numerous to count, and from the despair, I find myself whispering

"Let it rise."

Gratitude <3

2021

Sometimes there are no photographs, only
memories.
Sometimes there are no words, only emotions.
Sometimes the sweat is replaced with tears.
Sometimes the whispers turn into empty
intentions.
Sometimes who you wait for doesn't exist.
Sometimes who you can rely on is really just
yourself.
Sometimes the friendship turns into strangers.
Sometimes the world stops just to continue on
again.
Sometimes you just need to be reminded

To love,
Honor,
And respect -

Yourself.

2022

I sat
And looked at all the pieces
That had fallen to the floor

I'm confused
There should be more
And definitely jagged
Darker
And painful

Puzzled
Trying to figure it out
Finally realizing
Some became so light
They actually drifted away

Which left me
Open
Free
But consequently

Vulnerable
To forgotten
And misdiagnosed
Predators

So I embraced it
Wrapped myself in it
Accepted it
I'm not going to feed it
Encourage it
Or even like it
But.

I've pulled up a chair
Fluffed a pillow
Got a warm blanket
Even steeped in some tea
Mimicking self-love

I don't know the name
But it's familiar
I've pushed it away
Now I want to know it
Intimately understand

Hello
Heartbreak and boundaries
We meet again
We are just visitors
So should probably
Make the best of it
And just like always
We shall part soon

Past
Present
And future
Colliding into
The entangled duality of self.

Pisces

As I lay on his chest,
Heart beating and
Breath in unison.
I wonder -
Is this just a small sample
Of the millions of living things
Breathing with me in sync?
In rhythm.
In peace.
As one.

Farewell

I saw you.
For the first time
In years.

The same.
Arrogant.
Unevolved.
Stagnant.
Lost.
Little boy.

I held on.
For much longer than I should have.
Tolerated more than most.
Terrified that I would let go too soon.
I hoped better for you.
Wanted more for you.
Wished.
Still do.

I think I was in love
With your potential
Instead of
Accepting
What was staring at me

In the face.

I'm not angry.
Not bitter.
Just sad.
Perhaps disappointed.
I deserve more.
And this
Isn't fair to me.
Never was.

I see you.
Struggling.
Reaching out.
Needing.
I can't help you.
Simply don't have the time.
Quite frankly, wasted enough.

And is it odd?
That I feel guilty
For flourishing
Being successful
And surpassing every expectation
That I ever had of myself?
Literally, blooming.
I love me more.
And am done
Holding myself back

Sacrificing
Giving
For others.

So I bid you farewell.
Wish you the best of luck.
The irony now is
The only regret
Is that I didn't let you go
To water my own flowers

Sooner.